Where Mind Feels & Heart Thinks

Emotional Intovert

Made with ❤ on the BookLeaf Publishing Platform
www.bookleafpub.in
www.bookleafpub.com

Dedication

Dedicated to my Parents, My sister kavisha , My brother shubham , My best friends ...

Preface

The emotions gathered here are just the struggles , pain, love we go through as an individual on a daily basis. It has the soul crushing & soul building experiences which makes the book unique.

Acknowledgements

Life comes at a full circle when God gives an opportunity to reflect at all the significant moments in human beings' life. This is one such opportunity where I would like to pay respects and gratitude to My Father **Prahlad Ramwani,** Mother **Priyanka Ramwani,** my little sister **Kavisha Ramwani** & brother **Shubham Ramwani** who has always been my confidante. These people are my strongest support system and have lived every Joyous and Sad moments without whom I would never have the strength to pursue this perilous yet wonderful Journey. I would also like to thank my Best friends **Dr. Jinal Upadhyay & Dr. Parth Damor** Who have always been there for constant support & trust .

1. My special one

You meet several people while you live,
some manage to leave their imprints more than you give
..
some begin when you do,
and some join in latter too.
But those who be till end,
Is the relationship u don't want to bend.
As those are the persons with whom you speak your
heart,
without considering or scared to be judged of any sort.
Though initially you misunderstand the imprints as
ordinary one,
But then you know that is a crucial one..
Because they are there when you are not with oneself,
To make you realize , every bit of urself.

2. Righteously wrong

Sometimes everything seems right,
then what went incorrect.
If it was for everyone's happiness,
Then why tears covered with heavy hearts.
If it was planned for future,
Then why the hell bias for the present.
If it was for pride ,
Then why it feels like a humiliation.
If it was for the reasons,
Then why nothing could be justified.
If it was to calm the chaos,
Then why it created more havoc than ever.

3. Just

Everything to be in optimal amount.
Just the sufficient of heat , to burn the hesitations.
Just the overwhelming rain , to wash out the worst
flashbacks.
Just the satisfactory heartbreak is needed , to bring out
the strongest .
Just the mesmerizing pain, to accomplish your best
version .
Just the reasonable amount of tears , to reveal the
concealed.
Just the adorable anxiety , to value the peace within.
Just the impressive chaos, to silent the inner mess.

4. Horrendous

On that horrific night,
I never had the insight,
That next morning would not be in my sight.
When I heard the unusual footsteps,
never knew it would be a tough fight.
then was covered with evil hand on my mouth,
So that I cannot shout.
Salt coursed my broken body , over scratches with the
horrendous scream not heard aloud.
Was covered with corrupt hands at every part without
any doubt,
 Brutality was at the peak that every part was bleeding
in a bout.
Still , this did not stopped them & continued with
ferrocity,
To the point that the struggling heart & distressing mind
lost to this attrocity.
Though after this tough fight,
People still have the question , why I was at that site.
Little did I knew that it was my last night.
But one thing that came in the light
If the mentality does not change there will be another
moumita in the plight...

5. Expectations

Expectations are the pervasive myth,
Which compels you to live with.
It makes your heart to long for,
Clouds the brain to act as never before.
It grows the hope and holds on,
One that has already passed on.
So let your heart learn to let go,
And find peace in the present flow,
As least one wants to know,
That you suffered deeply in your low.

6. Woman

A female is always thought to be soft person,
But if u dig in deep , you won't find more braver than
one.
When you see her , you would always find her with a
smile.
But at one of her corner , she is crying for a
while.
Like two side of a coin, while walking in sun
You would never notice the pain
 in her loin.
Always underrate for the work they do,
But its a bet if anyone can walk
in their shoe.
For the immense trauma they can bear,
Is evident by letting their body tear.

7. Emotions

Emotions make us truly alive,
Tears, essential to survive,
Yet branded as weakness, a fragile facade,
While smiles are demanded, an unending charade,
Even as joy struggles to thrive.
Love's hope rewards those who strive,
But anger stands ready, a constant beside.

8. Best friend

A soul whose wisdom knows no bound,
Yet flows like peace on revered ground.
Patience, a sea of grace,
Perseverance, time cannot erase.
A friend who has the listening ear,
With a heart to believe & mind to endure.
A constant star in darkest night,
Guiding you towards the light.

9. Equity

It just starts from the womb,
To be prepared for doom.
Deemed to be perfect,
Fairness is always kept checked,
Substandard tranditions walk behind,
Plumpy or slim are just declined.
Emotions shown, a needy plea,
Emotions held, a heart's decree.
Words unleashed, a sharp attack,
 Words withheld, a silent crack.
A constant war, within the soul,
To fit the mold, or break the whole.

10. Let go

Humans have tendency to hold back,
A self made prison, a significant setback.
Still heart loves the continous attacks,
With mind struggles with flashbacks,
And soul has strayed from the track.
But life has different soundtrack,
Teaches you to smile at every smack.
It goes on waiting for your comeback,
But without letting go ,you'll find yourself going back.

11.

Humans have tendency to hold back,
A self made prison, a significant setback.
Still heart loves the continous attacks,
With mind struggles with flashbacks,
And soul has staryed from the track.
But life has different soundtrack,
Teaches you to smile at every smack.
It goes on waiting for your comeback,
But without letting go ,you'll find yourself going back.

11. Its ok

Its ok to be ,not ok
Its ok to let the tears purify the soul,
Its ok to shout out to calm the inside,
Its ok to have a heartbreak to trust the least,
Its ok to have a restless sleep , in a hope of better
mornings,
It is just not ok to ignore your self worth, that is what
needed.....

12. Need

13

We need everything
Storms are needed to stand still at all possible outcomes,
Rains are needed to make you realize that to cry is not a
sin
Thunder is needed to express yourself   at best possible
way,
Lightning to reignite the inner spark within you,
Heat is needed to make you realize that hardwork pays
you well.

13. The Repeat

I m sry if I call u so much
I m sry if I msg u so much
I m sry if I irritate u so much
I m sry if I have uncontrol tears for u
I m sry if I had hurt u anytime
I m sry if I m forcing u to be with me
I m sry if I could not see a tear in your eye
I m sry if I love u
I m sry If I Die without telling u

14. Heartbreak

Not everything is complete,
Because the imperfection has its beauty.
Not every beginning has the end ,
Some lose it the mid way for the other way out..
Not every journey has the destination,
for some they teach the way to it.
Not every wish is fulfilled,
Some are there to remain for a hope to live .
Not everytime you can have success or the failure,
Success & failure , nothing is ultimate.
Not all love unite at the end ,
It takes your soul , to be together in the worst.

15. Peace

Once I saw a girl,
That chose to be different,
Although there were times,
She was all alone, and hurt,
But she chose to smile,
Like meadow in desert,
That chose to survive in midst of all pain,
Though all her pain was unnoticed,
Her eyes still searches for peace that awaits her,
She knew this was only way,
One that she never wanted,
But deep down she knew,
It made her better nd
There she was,
Ready to battle anything,
That stands her way.....

16. Pain

The pain cuts so deep, which numbs the soul,
Leaving feelings dormant, beyond control.
Tears stream freely, a silent tide,
Transforming life to a hollow shell inside.

Self-trust erodes, a fragile, broken thing,
Each hesitant step, a wavering swing.
Solitude offers no solace, no release,
Just the heavy burden of inner unease.

The body betrays, a vessel out of sync,
The mind in shadows, on despair's dark brink.
A detached soul, adrift and lost at sea,
Longing for peace, longing to be free.

17. Resilience

You have to let go of people who are just okay with
loosing you,
You have to be thankful for the friendship , who holds
you from falling.
You need to stop thinking for people who never
even bothered .
You have to praise the time, who brought the boldness
within.
You dont have to weep, who were effortless to you.
But need to adore your heart , for it to be so patient.

18. Hope

When trust is delusional,
Respect appears unsual,
Guilt becomes unstoppable,
Love occurs conditional,
Suffering exist incredible,
Acceptance , a locked door,
& hate, a raging fire in the soul,
Yet even there a whisper of hope remains .

19. Love

Love transcends the need for marriage's hold,
Unbound by any stage, its story's told.
You can love deeply, simply being you,
Even when distance keeps your loved one from view,
When your affection rings genuinely true.

20. Concise

Not where you reach ,
But where you begin matters.
So just disbelieve,
When wholesome 'society' flatters.
But take the word,
If your loved ones are shatter.
Bcos only those,
Are with you till the end,
Rest just pretend.